DOCTOR WHO

The Eleventh Hour

Written by Trevor Baxendale
Based on the television script 'The Eleventh Hour' by Steven Moffat

BBC

Published by Pearson Education Limited, Edinburgh Gate, Harlow, Essex, CM20 2JE
Registered company number: 872828

www.pearsonschools.co.uk

Text © Pearson Education 2011

Designed by www.arnosdesign.co.uk

BBC (word mark and logo) is a trade mark of the British Broadcasting Corporation and are used under licence.

The right of Trevor Baxendale to be identified as author of this work has been asserted by him in accordance with the Copyright, Designs and Patents Act 1988.
The Eleventh Hour is based on the television script 'The Eleventh Hour' by Steven Moffat.

First published 2011

2020
10 9 8 7

British Library Cataloguing in Publication Data
A catalogue record for this book is available from the British Library

ISBN 978 1 408 27411 8

Copyright notice
All rights reserved. No part of this publication may be reproduced in any form or by any means (including photocopying or storing it in any medium by electronic means and whether or not transiently or incidentally to some other use of this publication) without the written permission of the copyright owner, except in accordance with the provisions of the Copyright, Designs and Patents Act 1988 or under the terms of a licence issued by the Copyright Licensing Agency, Saffron House, 6–10 Kirby Street, London EC1N 8TS (www.cla.co.uk). Applications for the copyright owner's written permission should be addressed to the publisher.

Printed and bound at Ashford Colour Press

Acknowledgements
We would like to thank the children and teachers of Bangor Central Integrated Primary School, NI; Bishop Henderson C of E Primary School, Somerset; Brookside Community Primary School, Somerset; Cheddington Combined School, Buckinghamshire; Cofton Primary School, Birmingham; Dair House Independent School, Buckinghamshire; Deal Parochial School, Kent; Newbold Riverside Primary School, Rugby and Windmill Primary School, Oxford for their invaluable help in the development and trialling of the Bug Club resources.

Every effort has been made to contact copyright holders of material reproduced in this book. Any omissions will be rectified in subsequent printings if notice is given to the publishers.

Contents

Prologue	4
Chapter 1	6
Chapter 2	10
Chapter 3	15
Chapter 4	19
Chapter 5	24
Chapter 6	28
Chapter 7	32
Chapter 8	37
Chapter 9	41
Chapter 10	47
Chapter 11	50
Chapter 12	54
Chapter 13	58
Chapter 14	62

PROLOGUE

The TARDIS, the Doctor's time machine, was out of control.

Inside, the Doctor struggled to regain control of the machine.

There was no time to think about that now. The TARDIS was on a collision course with the planet Earth. Ignoring the flames and sparks around him, the Doctor grabbed the central console and tried to bring the time machine back under his command.

The TARDIS hurtled through the atmosphere of Earth, flashing over continents like a stone skimming over water. It finally hit the ground with a shattering roar in the back garden of a nine-year-old girl called Amelia Pond.

CHAPTER 1

Amelia Pond was worried. There was a crack in her bedroom wall. It wasn't an ordinary crack. It was long and slightly curved, like a crooked smile. It gave her the creeps.

Every night, Amelia wished for someone to come and fix the crack. Not a builder – the crack was too strange for that. She needed someone to investigate it, to work out what it meant. A police officer, perhaps.

Then one night – *CRASH!*

Amelia jumped. Something had just landed in her back garden.

She ran downstairs and outside. The garden shed had been flattened and sitting on top of the wreckage was a large blue box. The box was smoking and lying on its side. Amelia could see a sign above the windows that said: POLICE PUBLIC CALL BOX.

The doors of the police box crashed open and a man slowly climbed out. He had thick brown hair hanging down over a pair of deep-set eyes. His clothes were ragged and he looked rather dazed. Amelia didn't know yet that the man was a Time Lord – someone who travelled in time around the universe fighting evil, dangerous beings. He caught sight of Amelia and his eyes brightened.

"Can I have an apple?" he asked.

Amelia frowned.

"Are you a policeman?" she asked, glancing back at the sign on the box.

"Why? Did you call a policeman?"

"Have you come about the crack in my wall?"

The Doctor looked at her curiously. "Does it scare you?"

"Yes."

"Well, then!" The man jumped to his feet and clapped his hands together. "Let's get on with it. I'm the Doctor. I've come to help you, so do everything I tell you, and don't wander off!"

They went into Amelia's house and the Doctor declared that he was hungry. He helped himself to an apple. He took one bite and then spat it out.

"Ugh! Hate apples! Got any yoghurt?"

Amelia found some yoghurt in the fridge.

The Doctor took one spoonful and spat that out too. He tried bacon, beans, even bread and butter – but they were all disgusting to him.

Then the Doctor suddenly realised what he really wanted. Fish fingers and custard!

Amelia sat and watched as the Doctor ate them with relish. He drank the last of the custard straight from the bowl, leaving a thick custardy moustache on his lip. He wiped it off with his hand. He certainly seemed like an odd doctor.

"What's your name?"

"Amelia Pond."

"Good name. Like something from a fairy tale."

Amelia had never thought about it before, but she liked the idea. The Doctor asked her more questions and discovered that Amelia lived alone with her aunt, who was out at the moment.

"I'm not scared of anything," Amelia told him.

"Not even the crack in your wall?" he asked.

CHAPTER 2

The Doctor examined the crack in the wall very carefully. Amelia watched as he traced the long, crooked smile with his fingertips.

"It doesn't go all the way through the wall," he said thoughtfully. He rummaged in his pocket and pulled something out. It looked like a silver pen with a blue bulb at one end. The Doctor pointed it at the wall. The tip of the device glowed and a shrill whine filled the air.

"What's that?" Amelia asked.

"Sonic screwdriver. This is a very special crack, Amelia. If you knocked this wall down, the crack would still be there." The Doctor switched off the screwdriver. "This crack is *not* in the wall. It's in everything. Two parts of space and time that should never have touched."

The Doctor leaned closer to the wall and listened carefully.

"Prisoner Zero has escaped!" boomed a voice from the far side. The Doctor jumped back.

"What does that mean?" wondered Amelia nervously.

"It means that there's a prison on the other side of this wall," replied the Doctor. "One of the prisoners has got away."

The crack suddenly yawned wide open.

The Doctor peered into it. "Hello? Hello?"

Suddenly, a giant eyeball appeared in the crack, staring out at the Doctor and Amelia. It was as if it were looking for something.

"Where is Prisoner Zero? Prisoner Zero has escaped!" boomed the voice again.

The Doctor was fascinated. "Prisoner Zero has escaped," he repeated thoughtfully.

A bell started to clang outside. It sounded like some kind of alarm. Amelia had never heard anything like it before, but the Doctor obviously had.

A look of horror crossed his face and then he sprinted out of Amelia's room, downstairs, through the kitchen and out into the garden.

Amelia raced after him. He was heading for the old box that had landed in the garden.

"Oh no!" the Doctor wailed. "The engines are going to burn!"

"It's just an old police box," protested Amelia. "How can a box have engines?"

"It's not a box. It's a time machine!"

Amelia looked at the police box again. A time machine? She so wanted to believe him. Why else would this funny man be so worried about an old box?

The Doctor was already climbing back into it. "Just a five-minute hop into the future should fix it. I'll be right back." He turned back to look at Amelia and smiled warmly. "Trust me – I'm the Doctor!"

The police box doors snapped shut behind him and then, with a great wheezing and groaning noise, the Doctor's time machine disappeared into thin air.

Five minutes, thought Amelia.

She dashed back into the house. If the Doctor had a time machine, then she wanted to see it. She wanted a ride in it! So she packed an overnight bag, fetched her coat and hat, and ran back out into the garden.

She sat down by the ruins of the shed and waited for the Doctor to come back.

She waited ... and waited ... for what seemed like for ever ...

CHAPTER 3

The TARDIS reappeared in the back garden of Amelia Pond's house. It was upright this time but still surrounded by a cloud of smoke.

The Doctor burst out and ran back towards the house.

"Amelia!" he yelled, sprinting through the back door and up the stairs. "Prisoner Zero is still here!"

The Doctor banged on Amelia's bedroom door. He was worried. She could be in terrible danger. "Amelia! Amelia?"

CLICK!

Metal handcuffs snapped shut around one of his wrists. There was a young policewoman standing behind him. She fastened the other end of the handcuffs to a radiator. There was no escape.

The Doctor looked at the policewoman. She reminded him of someone.

"You've been caught breaking and entering," said the policewoman severely.

The Doctor frowned. He didn't remember it like that at all. "Wait a minute! Where's Amelia?"

"Amelia?"

"Yes. Little girl. Red hair. Left her here about five minutes ago. The engines were burning, you see." The Doctor considered. "I think I may have gone a little too long. I promised her five minutes."

The policewoman stared intently at the Doctor. "Amelia Pond hasn't lived here for a long time."

Now the Doctor was starting to get worried again. "How long? Look, I need to speak to whoever owns this house. It's important."

"It's my house," said the policewoman icily.

"I thought you were the police?"

"I am. This is where I live. Have you got a problem with that?"

The Doctor's eyes narrowed. "How many rooms are there up here?"

"What?"

"How many rooms? Count them."

"Why?"

"Because it will change your life."

Puzzled, she quickly counted the doors to all the rooms leading from the landing. "Five. There are five rooms."

"Six."

"What?"

"There are six rooms – including that one behind you, the one you never see."

Slowly, the policewoman turned to look at the door at the far end of the landing. How could she have not noticed it before?

"There's a perception filter all around the door," explained the Doctor. "There's something hiding in that room. It's been there a long time. Whatever it is, it's created the filter to make someone see only what it wants them to see."

The policewoman started to walk towards the door.

"Don't touch that door!" the Doctor commanded. Too late – the policewoman walked into the darkened room beyond.

CHAPTER 4

The room was cold. It smelled strange, like rotting flowers.

"Get out of there!" called the Doctor.

The policewoman could see nothing to be afraid of. Then, silent and unseen, it slithered down behind her – a huge, glistening grey snake with a mouth full of long, needle-sharp fangs. It hung behind her, its flat yellow eyes level with the back of her head. Every time she turned around the snake moved as well, staying out of sight.

"There ... nothing here," she said.

"There is something in there," the Doctor called. "But you mustn't try to see it. If it knows you've seen it, it will kill you."

The policewoman shivered. Then, as she turned quickly, she saw it. The snake's huge jaws gaped open and the fangs drooled.

She ran straight out, slammed the door and headed for the Doctor.

"What was that thing?" she demanded.

"An inter-dimensional multi-form from outer space," came the instant reply. The Doctor tugged at the handcuffs. "Come on, where's the key to these? We need to go."

"I lost it," said the policewoman still staring at the door. "What's that thing doing in my house?"

"I don't know." The Doctor glanced up at her. "Run. Just go. I'll be all right. Call in some backup on your police radio."

"There is no backup," said the woman. "It's a pretend radio. I'm not a real policewoman. I'm going to a fancy dress party."

The Doctor was about to say something else when the door of the cold, dark room crashed open and a man came out with a large dog on a chain.

The woman gasped. Was she going mad? First the room hadn't existed at all. Then it did exist and there was some kind of weird space-snake inside it. Now there was a man and a dog!

They were both growling. Then the man started barking. Not the dog. The man.

"Clever old multi-form," said the Doctor. His eyes were shining with curiosity. "It's all one creature but disguised as two. Just got the voice a bit mixed up."

The man snarled at him.

"You must have based yourself on someone real though," said the Doctor. "Where did you get it? You'd need some kind of psychic link …"

The man with the dog snarled again and this time bared his teeth – or rather, his fangs. His mouth was full of the same sharp, needle-like teeth that the space-snake had shown off.

Suddenly, the air was filled with a deep, booming voice, *"Attention, Prisoner Zero! The human residence is surrounded."*

"What's that?" asked the woman nervously.

"Something trying to capture the prisoner," replied the Doctor. "Which means we're safe."

"Prisoner Zero will vacate the human residence," boomed the voice. *"Or the human residence will be incinerated!"*

"Well," said the Doctor. "Safe apart from being burned alive."

CHAPTER 5

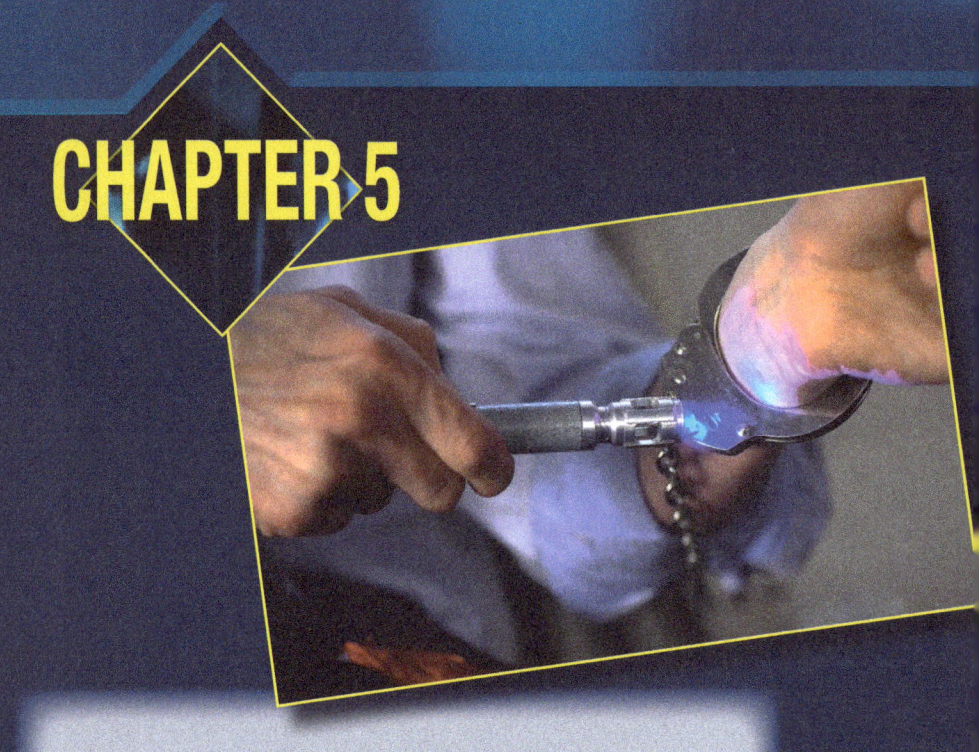

"Prisoner Zero will vacate the human residence," boomed the voice again. "Or the human residence will be incinerated!"

The Doctor was frantically trying to get his sonic screwdriver to work. He banged it on the floor until it began to glow. As soon as the handcuffs were unlocked, he grabbed the woman's hand, raced down the stairs and out into the garden.

The huge voice rang out, "Prisoner Zero will vacate the human residence or the human residence will be incinerated!"

"Will you please tell me what is going on?" demanded the woman.

"An alien convict called Prisoner Zero is hiding in your spare room disguised as a man and a dog," the Doctor replied. "Other aliens – the voice that we keep hearing – are trying to capture Prisoner Zero and are about to burn your house. Any more questions?"

They reached the TARDIS. The woman stared at it as the Doctor tried to unlock the door and failed. "No!" he wailed. "Don't do this, not now! It's still rebuilding itself – not letting us in!"

The man and the dog appeared at the window of the house. The man was barking fiercely.

"Come on!" The woman grabbed the Doctor and pulled him away from the police box. They had to get away.

The Doctor hung back, looking at the garden shed.

"No, wait. The shed. Wasn't it smashed to pieces when the TARDIS landed on it?"

"It's a new shed," said the woman impatiently. "Let's go!"

"It doesn't look new," observed the Doctor.

"Well it was once! You said you'd be back in *five minutes!*" shouted the woman angrily. It was as if years of frustration had suddenly burst out. "Five minutes? That was twelve years ago!"

The Doctor stared at her in shock. "You're Amelia," he realised. "You're the little girl – but you've grown up."

"I am Amelia and you're late."

The man and the dog were now at the back door, still barking furiously.

Amelia dragged the Doctor out of the garden.

"You're twelve years late," she snapped. "No one believed you really existed. Everybody said you were just my imagination."

Suddenly, the alien voice boomed out of every mobile phone and speaker system in the area. *"Prisoner Zero will vacate the human residence or the human residence will be incinerated!"* People looked all around them. They were too confused to be afraid. What did the strange message mean?

"Prisoner Zero will vacate the human residence or the human residence will be incinerated!"

CHAPTER 6

The Doctor ran into the nearest house, closely followed by Amelia. Inside, an elderly lady, Amelia's neighbour, was trying to switch channels on her TV, but every station was the same:

"Prisoner Zero will vacate the human residence or the human residence will be incinerated!"

On the TV screen was a giant eyeball – the same eyeball that had peered out through the crack in Amelia's bedroom wall twelve years ago.

"Hello!" said the Doctor. "Sorry to burst in."

The old lady looked curiously at the Doctor. He was still in his raggedy clothes and looked rather odd. She turned to Amelia.

"Hello, Amy," said the old lady. "Who's your friend?"

"Who's Amy?" asked the Doctor. "You were Amelia."

"Yeah, now I'm Amy."

"Amelia Pond – but that was a great name!"

"Bit *fairy tale*, don't you think?" Amy reminded him.

The Doctor looked closely at Amy. "What happened to you? You were a little girl five minutes ago!"

Amy sighed. "You're worse than my aunt."

"I'm the Doctor. I'm worse than everybody's aunt!" He smiled warmly at the old lady and then turned back to the TV. Using his sonic screwdriver, he switched through several foreign channels. The message about Prisoner Zero was repeated on every one. "OK, so it's in every language. They're broadcasting to the whole world."

The Doctor dashed over to the window, opened it and gazed up at the sky.

"What's up there? What are you looking for?" asked Amy. The Doctor didn't reply. The sky was empty. He came back inside, thinking aloud.

"OK. Planet this size, two poles, your basic molten core ... They're going to need a forty per cent fission blast but they're going to have to power-up first. So assuming it's a medium-sized starship, it'll take them twenty minutes to get here."

A tall young man called Jeff came into the house, carrying a laptop under one arm. He was rather puzzled to find a tatty-looking stranger in his gran's front room.

The Doctor looked at Jeff. "We've got twenty minutes," he said.

"Twenty minutes to what?"

The giant eyeball was still staring out of the screen. It repeated the now familiar message over and over, *"Prisoner Zero will vacate the human residence or the human residence will be incinerated!"*

"The human residence," repeated the Doctor. "They're not talking about your house, or anybody else's house. They're talking about the planet. Somewhere up there, there's a spaceship."

The Doctor pointed upwards. "They're going to incinerate the planet."

CHAPTER 7

There was indeed a spaceship. It was shaped like a giant snowflake and hovered above the Earth.

At the centre of the snowflake was an enormous eye. It was the same eye that the Doctor and Amy had first glimpsed through the crack in her bedroom wall twelve years ago, and which now stared out of every TV screen and computer monitor on the planet.

It peered into the deepest oceans and over the highest mountains, searching, searching …

"Prisoner Zero will vacate the human residence or the human residence will be incinerated!"

The Doctor knew he had twenty minutes to save the planet, but he didn't know where to start. He and Amy left Jeff and his gran in their house.

"What is this place?" the Doctor asked, as they walked down the high street.

"Leadworth." Amy was rather proud of the little village where she had grown up.

"Where's the rest of it?" asked the Doctor.

"This is it."

"Is there an airport?"

"No."

"A nuclear power station?"

"No."

"Not even a little one?"

Amy shook her head. "No."

"Nearest city?"

"Gloucester – half an hour away by car."

"We don't have half an hour, or a car," said the Doctor tersely. He paused outside the Post Office. "Twenty minutes to save the world and all I've got is a Post Office – and it's shut!"

The sky suddenly went dark, as if a great cloud had crossed the sun. Broad daylight turned into an eerie twilight.

"What's happening?" asked Amy. "Why's it going dark?"

The sun seemed to be a strange, dirty yellow colour.

"What's happened to the sun?" Amy demanded.

"Nothing," replied the Doctor. "You're looking at it through a force-field. The alien spaceship has sealed off your upper atmosphere and now it's getting ready to boil the planet."

People were coming out of shops and houses, and staring up at the darkened sun. Many were taking pictures of it on their mobile phones.

"Hang on, wait," said the Doctor. "I just saw something. What was it?"

34

He scanned the village green. His eyes flicked from one person to the next as they all stood looking up at the sky, mobile phones out to capture the image for ever.

There was one person who wasn't looking up at the sky. One person was aiming his camera phone at something else entirely. It was a young male nurse and he was taking a picture of a man and his dog. A man and a dog that were only too familiar to the Doctor and Amy. The multi-form!

The Doctor whirled round to face Amy, a new look of determination on his face. "Twenty minutes," he said. "Twenty minutes to save the world. I can do it."

Amy was unsure. She wanted to believe the Doctor. She wanted to believe that this was the same man she had last seen twelve years ago when she was nine years old and scared of a crack in her bedroom wall.

"Who are you really?" she asked. She had believed in him then, and in his stupid police box, but now ...?

"I'm the Doctor. I'm a time traveller. Everything I told you twelve years ago is true." He stared into her eyes, willing her to believe in him.

Amy knew it was true. She had waited for the Doctor to return for so long.

Suddenly, Amy felt nine years old again.

"What do we do?" she asked him. The Doctor grinned.

"Stop that nurse!"

CHAPTER 8

The Doctor sprinted across the village green, skidded to a halt by the male nurse, and grabbed his mobile phone.

"The sun's going out and you're photographing that man and his dog," said the Doctor. "Why?"

Amy caught up and the male nurse smiled at her. "Hello, Amy!"

"Hi," said Amy. She obviously knew him well. She introduced him quickly to the Doctor. "This is Rory. He's a friend."

"The man and his dog," the Doctor repeated. "Why?"

"Because he can't be here," said Rory. "He's in hospital, in a coma. I'm his nurse."

The Doctor smiled. "I knew it! A multi-form disguises itself as anything. It just needs a psychic link with a sleeping mind. Someone in a coma would be perfect."

The man and the dog barked suddenly. Above the village, the spaceship appeared.

The Doctor marched towards the man and his dog. "Prisoner Zero," he said. "That spaceship is looking for you. It's scanning the whole area for something alien."

Prisoner Zero growled.

The Doctor smiled. "Well, there's nothing so alien as a sonic screwdriver." He pointed the sonic screwdriver into the air. With one push of a button, every car, van and lorry engine started to roar, house alarms rang, lights flashed and sirens wailed.

Above them, the spaceship whirled around. Its giant eyeball scanned the village for the source of the sonic energy.

Just then, a shower of sparks burst out of the sonic screwdriver. It spluttered, then died.

Everything stopped. The spaceship's eye jerked back and forth, confused. The entire craft started to move away.

"No!" yelled the Doctor, looking up at the spaceship. "Come back! He's here! Prisoner Zero is here!"

The spaceship continued to move away. It flew higher into the sky, disappearing into the cloud.

The Doctor was furious. A perfect chance, lost because his sonic screwdriver had overloaded.

"Doctor! Look!" Amy was pointing at Prisoner Zero. The multi-form was giving up on its man-and-dog shape. It melted into a sludge-like mass and snaked its way down a nearby drain.

"It's gone!" gasped Rory.

"It's going to hide in human form again," said the Doctor. "We need to drive it out into the open so the alien spaceship can see it."

"How?" wondered Amy.

The Doctor bit his lip thoughtfully. "No TARDIS, no screwdriver, seventeen minutes left. Come on – think!"

CHAPTER 9

In Leadworth Hospital there was a special ward for coma victims – patients who were unconscious and had been for a long time. These people were perfect psychic links for the multi-form.

In one of the beds was a man named Barney. He appeared to be asleep. On the cabinet next to him was a photograph of him and his dog. This picture had given Prisoner Zero the pattern for its first human disguise.

Now that the disguise had been revealed, the multi-form had to move on. It had to stay one step ahead of the Doctor.

Emerging from an air vent inside the ward, the alien considered its next move …

On the village green, Amy Pond was struggling to understand what had been happening all her life. "So that alien hid in my house for twelve years?"

"Multi-forms can live for thousands of years," said the Doctor. "Twelve years is nothing."

"So how come they show up on the same day you do?"

"They're looking for Prisoner Zero but they followed me. They saw me through the crack, remember. They're only late because I am."

The Doctor thumbed through the photographs on Rory's phone, pausing at a picture of the man and his dog.

"These are all coma patients. This one dreams he's walking his dog and so Prisoner Zero gets a dog ... it's all down to the psychic link. We have to drive him out into the open. Or find a way of pointing him out to the spaceship."

Suddenly, he threw his arms around Rory and Amy. "Got it. You two, go into the hospital, go straight to the coma ward, clear everyone out. I'm going to find a laptop."

Then the Doctor raced off without another word.

"Come on!" Amy grabbed Rory and they headed off for the hospital.

The Doctor ran straight to Jeff's gran's house.

Jeff was busy with his laptop. He was surprised when the Doctor ran in and even more surprised when he grabbed the laptop and started to bash away at the keyboard.

Jeff's gran followed the Doctor into the room. "What's going on?"

"The sun's gone wibbly," explained the Doctor without looking up. "All the experts in the world are panicking. They'll be having an emergency meeting by phone. Do you know what they need?"

Jeff and his gran shook their heads.

"Me," answered the Doctor. "Ah, here they are! The big boys – NASA, Jodrell Bank, Tokyo Space Centre, even Patrick Moore."

The laptop screen filled up with images of scientists logging on for their emergency call. They looked concerned – especially when they picked up an image of the Doctor from Jeff's webcam.

"Who is this?"

"Here are my credentials," said the Doctor, fingers tapping away. "Fermat's Last Theorem, why electrons have mass, and my personal favourite – faster than light travel with diagrams and a joke."

The scientists were amazed. In the twinkling of an eye, the Doctor had solved three advanced technical impossibilities.

"That's right, I'm a genius," explained the Doctor. "Now, look at the sun. You're going to need all the help you can get."

The scientists were fascinated as the Doctor started to hit keys on Rory's mobile phone. "I'm writing a computer virus," he explained. "Very clever, super-fast. OK, I'm sending this to all your computers. Get everyone who works for you to send this everywhere. Email, text, Facebook, Twitter, whatever you've got."

"What does this virus do?" asked one of the scientists.

"It's a reset command. Anything with a chip will default to zero at exactly the same time. Good luck."

The Doctor snapped shut the laptop. "Thanks, Jeff. Gotta dash. Bye!"

Jeff and his gran watched, open-mouthed, as the Doctor sprinted out of the house.

CHAPTER 10

In Leadworth Hospital, all Amy and Rory could see were empty corridors. Something had already cleared the hospital of its staff and patients.

Rory was leading Amy towards the coma ward when a woman and two girls stepped into the corridor. The mother looked worried. She breathed a sigh of relief when she saw Amy in her police uniform.

"What happened?" Amy asked.

"There was a man with a dog," said the woman.

"The size of that dog!" said one of the little girls. "It just went mad, barking, attacking everyone ..."

Something was very odd. The little girl was speaking with her mother's voice.

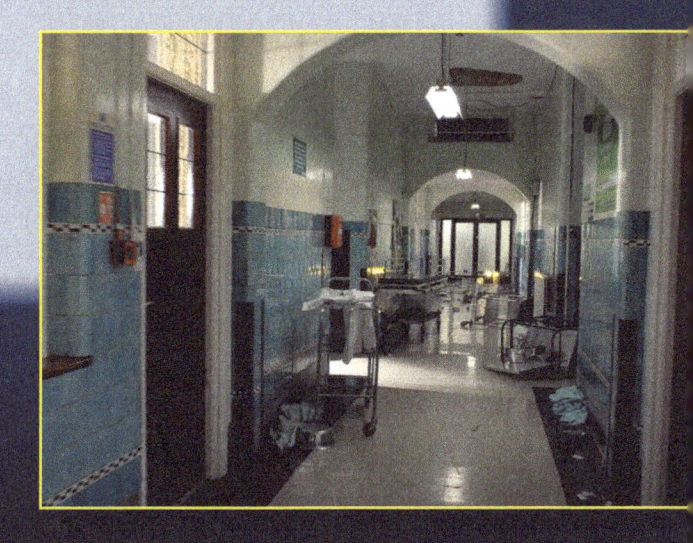

Amy and Rory stared at her. The little girl paused and the mother continued in exactly the same voice, "Oh, I'm getting it wrong again, aren't I? Too many mouths!"

She opened her mouth, revealing a huge set of sharp, needle-like fangs. It was Prisoner Zero, in another disguise.

Amy and Rory turned and ran, slamming the ward doors behind them. The multi-form raced after them.

Amy took out her mobile and dialled. She hoped the Doctor still had Rory's phone.

"Amy?" the Doctor's voice responded instantly. "Get out of the hospital – Prisoner Zero will be there!"

"It's here all right," replied Amy. "We're in the coma ward. It's trying to get in."

"Which window are you near?"

Amy frowned. What a strange question. "Fourth from the end. Far left. Why?"

The doors burst open. Prisoner Zero stepped into the ward, still looking like a mother with two little girls.

"Oh dear. Little Amelia Pond," said Prisoner Zero softly. "I've watched you grow up and you never even knew I was there. Little Amelia Pond, waiting for her magic Doctor to return. Well, he's too late this time!"

CHAPTER 11

The fourth window from the far left of the hospital ward suddenly opened and the Doctor jumped through. He flung his arms around Rory and Amy.

"Hello! Am I late?" He looked up at the digital clock above the doors. "No, still three minutes to go."

The Doctor turned to Prisoner Zero.

"Take off the disguise," he ordered. "They'll find you in a heartbeat and no one need die."

Prisoner Zero shook its human head. "The Atraxi will kill me this time, Doctor. If I'm to die, then this world will die with me."

"Look, you came to this world through a crack in space and time. Why don't you just leave the same way?"

"I didn't open the crack," said Prisoner Zero. "I cannot return."

Before the Doctor could respond, he was distracted by the clicking sound of the clock. He smiled. "We're off. Look at that."

The digits had turned to 0:00.

"Do you know what's happening right now?" asked the Doctor. "Thanks to Jeff's laptop and a computer virus, every digital clock, every radio display, every computer-controlled timer in the world is spreading the word. Do you know what the word is?"

Prisoner Zero frowned.

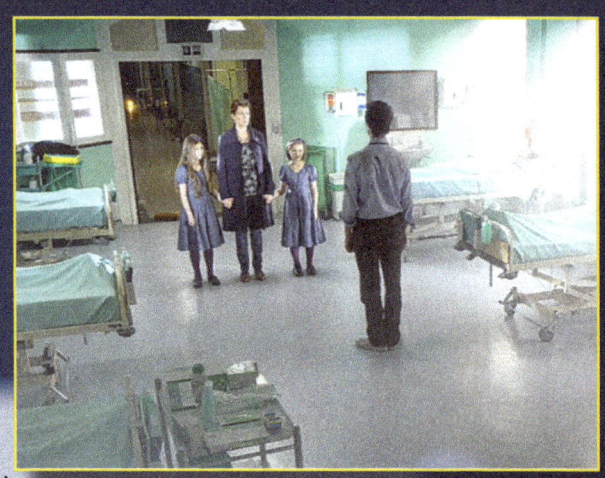

"The word is *zero*," said the Doctor. "Now, if I were up there in an Atraxi spaceship monitoring all Earth communications, I'd take that as a hint. I'd be able to track a virus to its source – right here."

The Doctor held up Rory's mobile phone.

A brilliant white light burst through the hospital windows. Amy and Rory ran to the window. The giant spaceship hovered outside, its eyeball swivelling as it searched the hospital.

"I think they just found us!" said the Doctor happily.

Prisoner Zero wasn't impressed. "The Atraxi have traced a phone, not me. They can't find me in my human disguise."

"Yeah, but this is the good bit. Do you know what this phone is full of? Pictures of you. Every form you've learned to take and I'm uploading them right now."

Prisoner Zero was speechless with rage.

"No TARDIS, no sonic screwdriver, two minutes to spare ... and I've beaten you." The Doctor grinned.

"I shall take a new form," said Prisoner Zero.

"You can't," replied the Doctor. "It takes months to build that kind of psychic link."

"Oh, I've had years." The woman with her two girls began to dissolve.

Then Amy Pond collapsed.

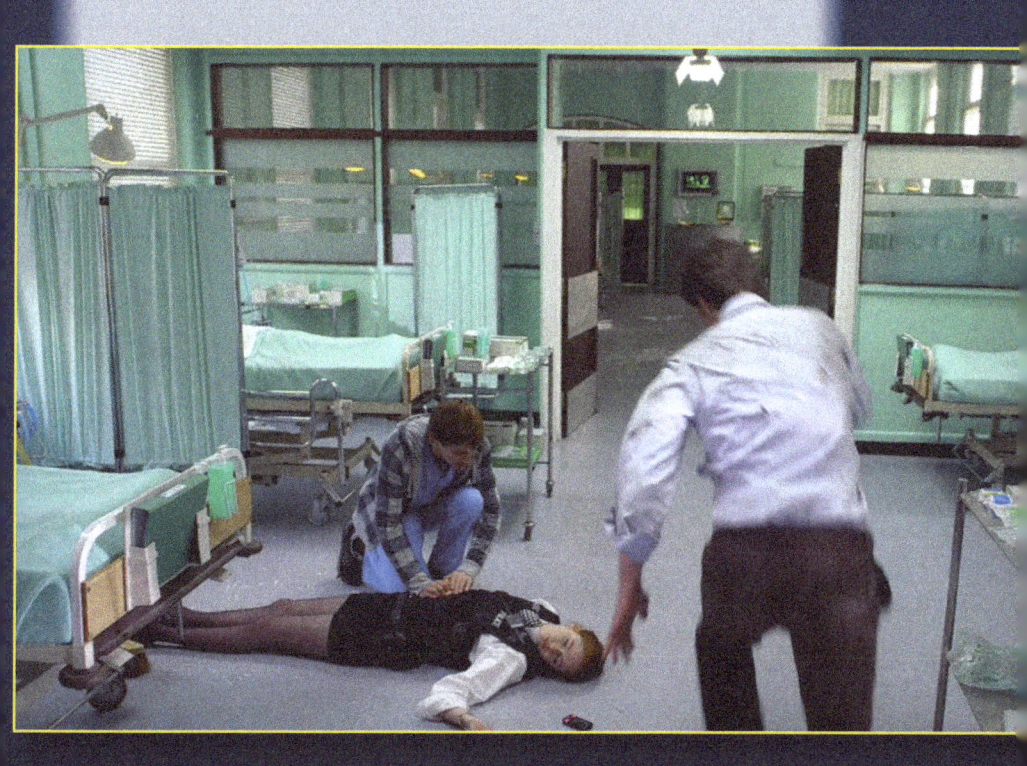

CHAPTER 12

The Doctor knelt over Amy.

"You've got to hold on, Amy," urged the Doctor. "Don't sleep! You've got to stay awake. Please!"

He looked up at Prisoner Zero. In the multi-form's place was a strange, young-looking man with a shock of unruly dark hair and penetrating, deep-set eyes. He wore raggedy clothes that desperately needed changing.

The Doctor frowned. "Well, that's rubbish. Who's that supposed to be?"

"It's you," said Rory.

The Doctor jumped to his feet and gazed at Prisoner Zero. It was like looking in a mirror. The multi-form had recreated his new face and body in perfect detail. "Why are you copying me?" asked the Doctor.

"I'm not," said a young girl's voice. Then Amelia Pond – the young, nine-year-old Amelia, or the perfect image of her – stepped out from behind the Prisoner Zero version of the Doctor. The multi-form again.

"Poor Amy Pond," said Prisoner Zero. "Dreaming about her magic Doctor who will return to save her. What a disappointment you've been."

"No," replied the Doctor. "She's dreaming about me because she can still hear me."

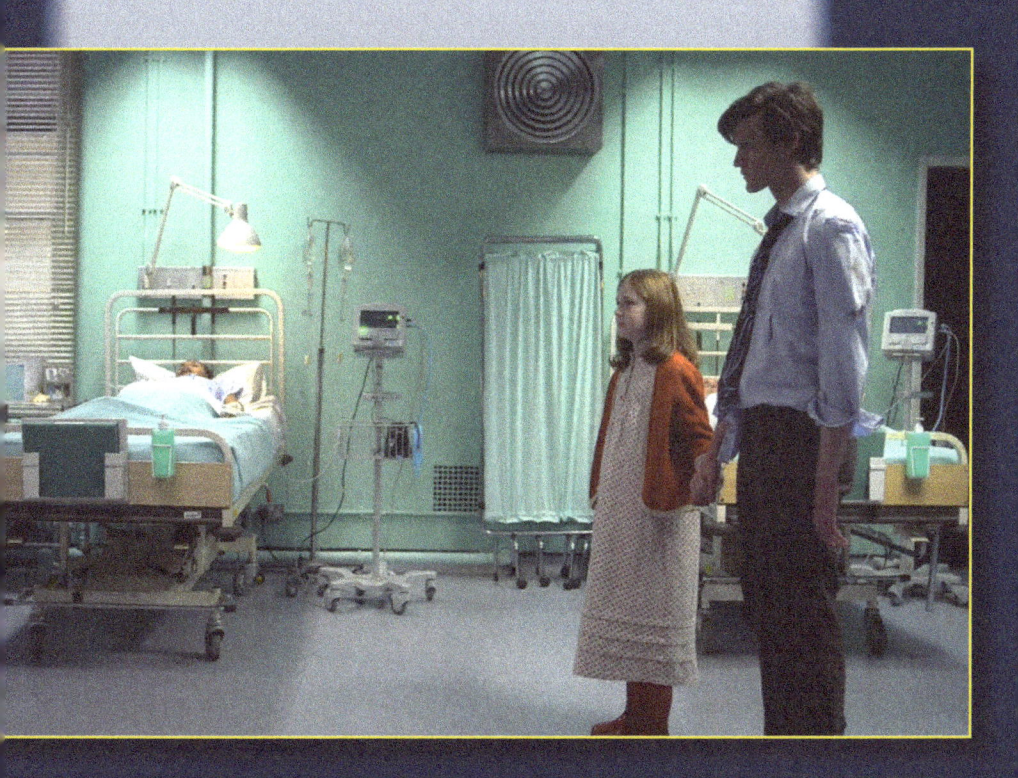

He dashed back to Amy. "Amy! I know you can hear me. Remember the room, the room in your house you couldn't see? Remember you went inside? Amy – *dream about what you saw in there.*"

"No!" Amelia Pond cried out. Or rather, Prisoner Zero did. Suddenly, it found itself changing back to its original alien form – the giant, writhing snake-like creature with sharp fangs and glowing eyes – the real image of Prisoner Zero that Amy's subconscious was now remembering.

"Well done, Prisoner Zero," said the Doctor. "A perfect impersonation of yourself."

"Prisoner Zero is located!" boomed a familiar voice. *"Prisoner Zero is restrained!"*

Then the alien snake vanished, teleported from the hospital straight into the Atraxi spaceship which was hovering above the building.

"The sun's back to normal," gasped Rory. "That means it's all over!"

"Not quite," the Doctor muttered. He held the mobile phone to his ear. It was still connected to the Atraxi spaceship. "Oi," he said. "No one said you could go. Did you think you could burn this planet and no one would notice? Wait there. I'm coming up to see you."

CHAPTER 13

The Doctor went up to the hospital roof, pausing on the way to rummage through a locker room full of clothes left by hospital staff. "If I'm saving the world, I need to look the part," he announced to Amy and Rory.

By the time they reached the roof, the Doctor had almost completely changed. Gone were the old raggedy clothes and worn-out trainers. In their place was a pair of smart boots, dark trousers and a shirt.

Hovering just above the hospital was the Atraxi spaceship. Amy and Rory shrank back.

"Is this a good idea?" Amy wondered. "Wouldn't it be better if you just let them leave?"

"Leaving is good," agreed the Doctor. "Never coming back is better."

He called up to the spaceship. "The Doctor will see you now!"

The eyeball lowered itself until it was level with the Doctor. A light scanned him and a familiar, booming voice spoke, *"You are not of this world."*

"No, but I've put a lot of work into it."

"Is this world important?"

"Important?" scoffed the Doctor. "Six billion *people* live here. Here's a better question: is this world protected? You're not the first lot to come here, you know. What you've got to ask is ... what do you think happened to the other visitors who came here like you? Who do you think protected the Earth then?"

The eyeball scanned the Doctor again. The Doctor had now finished putting on his outfit. The bow tie and tweedy jacket were an odd combination but somehow it suited him perfectly. The Atraxi saw who the Doctor really was – through all his ten different life-times, until he had become the man he was today.

The Eleventh Doctor.

"Yes, I'm the Doctor. Basically ... *run!*"

The eyeball shot back up into the spaceship, then the entire vessel turned and fled. Amy and Rory watched it shrink into a tiny frosty dot in the sky until it disappeared.

"Is that it?" asked Amy. "Have they gone?" She turned.

The Doctor had also gone.

Amy and Rory caught up with the Doctor back at the house. The blue police box was still standing in the back garden and the Doctor was just disappearing inside.

A strange wheezing and groaning sound filled the air, a sound Amy had not heard for twelve long years. The last time she'd heard it, the same thing had happened. The police box, the Doctor's time machine, had disappeared.

It was doing the same thing again.

CHAPTER 14

Two years passed before Amy Pond heard that sound again. It was the middle of the night. She leaped out of bed and ran downstairs in her dressing gown.

The TARDIS was back in her garden, light shining from its windows. Standing in front of it, smiling proudly, was the Doctor. He was still in his tweed jacket and bow tie, looking exactly as he had the last time Amy had seen him.

"Sorry about running off earlier," he told her breezily. "Brand new TARDIS! Bit exciting. Just had a quick hop to the moon and back to run her in. She's ready for the big stuff now."

"You came back," said Amy.

"Of course I came back. I always come back."

"You kept the clothes, even the bow tie."

"Yeah. Bow ties are cool."

Amy frowned in disbelief. "Are you from another planet?"

"Yeah. So what do you think? Other planets. Want to check some out?"

"Hang on, all that stuff in the hospital ... Prisoner Zero and the spaceship ..." began Amy.

"Oh, don't worry. That's just the beginning," replied the Doctor. "There's loads more."

"But all that stuff was two years ago!"

"Oops! Two years? That's fourteen years in total since fish custard." The Doctor bit his lip. "Still want to come with me? You did fourteen years ago."

Amy looked serious. "I grew up."

"Don't worry, I'll soon fix that." The Doctor clicked his fingers and the police box doors opened.

Amy could not resist. She stepped through the doors.

The TARDIS was huge inside. There were steps leading up to a control console bristling with strange instruments and pieces of equipment. The air hummed with power.

63

Amy ran to the controls, fascinated.

The Doctor joined her. "All of time and space … everything that ever happened and ever will …" He started to operate the controls and the TARDIS was filled with a familiar wheezing and groaning noise.

"Where do you want to start?"